CAREER MENTOR

Strategies for choosing a mentor for
Motivation, Inspiration and Success

WASEEM HYDER

Table of Contents

INTRODUCTION 4
CHAPTER ONE 5
   An Essential Guide to Career Mentoring 5
   The Advantages of Having A Career Mentor 7
   Why You Need a Career Mentor 8
   Finding a Career Mentor 10
CHAPTER TWO 19
   A Career Mentor – Help Advance a Career 19
   The Importance of Career Mentoring 22
   3 Tips for Choosing the Right Mentor to Advance Your Career 24
   Begin Advancing Your Career Today 25
CHAPTER THREE 28
   A Mentor Program Makes Great Sense! 28
   Step by step instructions to Find a Career Mentor 31
   Need a Good Mentor? Here's How to Find One 34
   How would you find one? 36
   Strategies for Choosing a Mentor for Motivation, Inspiration, and Success 38
CHAPTER FOUR 42
   Three Fundamental Mistakes To Avoid When Choosing A Mentor 42
   4 Secrets to Finding a Mentor Who's Perfect for You 44
   The Value of Having a Professional Mentor 46
   Simple Choosing the Right Career 48
CONCLUSION 52

INTRODUCTION

Make a success of your career; then a mentor is a great person to have on your team. They will have the experience and the advice to help develop your career. Help your chosen profession today by following this guide on finding mentors. For the uninitiated, let us first answer the questions: Who is a mentor? For what reason does one need a mentor or for what purpose would it be a good idea for one to endeavor to be one? Where to find a mentor? The answer to these questions would most likely open up more up to date openings in your mind as interchange career paths uncover themselves when you go further in the subject. A mentor is someone who is your guide, friend, and also savant in matters identified with your career, personal growth and advancement and also your own life. He or she counsels and prompts you not just when you are in an emergency circumstance yet also when you are the junction of life – be it any circumstance. The end product to your comprehension could be: What is in it for him? A mentor can pick up tremendously in his own life, as he/she holds the hand of someone who needs his assistance." We trust that there is no better apparatus in life which encourages you in your personal growth than to be a mentor to someone. You take a gander at this opportunity from the mentors' point of view; you do not just feel glad for the way that you are helping someone to achieve his particular inactive potential, however, have a great feeling of improved confidence when you see people depend on you for advice and direction.

CHAPTER ONE

An Essential Guide to Career Mentoring

Career mentoring isn't new. In the past times, mentoring was done as an apprenticeship. Hundreds of years back, before you could turn into a good smithy, you expected to work under an ace metal forger. These days, nonetheless, finding a mentor isn't essential for the vast majority. View yourself as fortunate on the off chance that you see a boss or manager who will confer a couple of subtle strategies to encourage your career. It appears that such vast numbers of managers or administrators feel debilitated by the people who are under them, that they tend to keep workers oblivious more often than not. Besides going to instructional classes, enhancing your skills, and adopting new things, a mentor will help set you up for the career way that you intend to take. Here is a portion of the things that you should think about mentoring.

You ought not to expect that your manager or direct chief will turn into your programme mentor. You can even have a career mentor that isn't working for your company. You can indeed ask your folks, instructors, relatives, and companions to be your mentor. If you need to climb the step of accomplishment in your office, it is smarter to find a mentor that works in a similar industry that you are trying to work inside. On the off chance that you can't see someone in your company who will offer a helping hand, you can join professional organizations or relationship as a way to find the correct mentor for you. In any case, you ought to recall not to get a mentor from your company's rivals, as this could be view as a clashing interest.

Meetings are not just important in conceptualizing, trading data, and discussing plans. Mentors additionally make utilization of meetings keeping in mind the end goal to guide the people under their wings. If your boss calls you for a one-on-one meeting, don't approach it with worry and dread. Typically, week by week 'one-on-ones' with your mentor or boss can enable you to all the more likely comprehend the targets of the company and the necessities of your work. It is likewise the time to allow your boss to become acquainted with you better and figure out how to confide in you with new assignments and more duties. Trust it or not, mentors additionally make utilization of group meetings to help certainty and enhance relational abilities of the people under them.

What are the characteristics of a good career mentor? To begin with, you have to search for someone who has immense experience and learning in your industry. Next, a good mentor is liberal and will grant to you his or her knowledge and insight. Additionally, guarantee that the mentor whom you will pick is someone who is resolved to end up your instructor and guide. It additionally helps if he or she knows how to impart exceptionally well.

Who is a Mentor? Discover a Mentor

Numerous people are either searching for a way to improve their career prospects or start another career without any preparation in the wake of leaving school or school. Indeed, even people leaving college may at present have no clue about what they need to improve the situation a career thus may end up requesting help.

When you are in your last long periods of school or school in Australia, you offered various career advice sessions; these are intended to make you consider what it is you need to do. Inconvenience is that they don't answer the numerous inquiries. On the off chance that you have a particular point in life then these summed up career sessions are not going to be of any utilization.

What is a career mentor?

A career mentor is a precious person to talk to, they are a personal coach, yet rather than getting your body into the shape they kick your career into shape. They go about as a helper, and an instructor, tuning in to your experiences and after that consoling you. A career mentor offers practical help as you can state anything you need to them without dread of them chuckling at you.

They are likewise entirely unprejudiced which will make the advice that you get considerably more essential and dependable. Most mentors are experiencing business people; most have numerous long stretches of experience. The ones that you will need to talk to are ones in either same business or a similar industry from yourself. You can likewise get career advice from your associates.

If you can locate a great career mentor then you can hope to get hold of some constructive and significant unprejudiced advice, they will likewise have the capacity to direct you through career alternatives and offer recommendations. These people can assist you with getting your foot in the entryway of a most loved job and get you to the interview. The coaching will likewise improve your chances of prevailing at the meeting and should make it more probable that you will land yourself a high position.

Finding a Career Mentor

Anybody can be a career mentor as it's merely actually someone to control you through your career and help you to decide which choices to make. By getting yourself a great career mentor, you can without much of a stretch to improve your job.

Extraordinary compared to other ways to discover a career mentor is to utilize destinations on the web; a standout amongst other is Career Savant. It is an excellent website intended to place people in contact with Australian specialists who know some things about the industry that you work. It should make it substantially less demanding to discover a mentor to enable you to decide what to do.

Career Savant makes it extremely simple to discover reliable career consultants found near your home with the goal that you can either talk to them on the telephone or even go to them to perceive what they need to state. You should pay for a mentor, however, its money well spent particularly when you consider it a more significant amount of speculation.

The Advantages of Having A Career Mentor

A career mentor is someone who goes about as an instructor, a spark, and a directing power in your career. It would be a person with whom you can talk uninhibitedly and from whom you can hope to get sound, fair-minded career advice. A mentor is usually a person who experienced, someone in your company or a similar industry who is higher in the pecking order, or someone whom you have worked with before and still offer a deep relationship.

A good mentor will in a perfect world give you unbiased advice, and also coach and guide you. Such a person is someone who won't just enable you to get a require the desired interview, yet will likewise allow you to perform well in such discussions and increment your chances of landing a good position.

Customarily, mentoring is something that you would not buy and would not require a financial trade. A mentor and a person mentored is far higher than what money can buy.

o It usually is useless to anticipate that your supervisor will be your mentor. An administrator and his youngsters, as a rule, have diverse interests while working towards a shared objective and it isn't best to tangle those interests in with a mentorship circumstance.

o Someone higher up in the company can all the more appropriately qualify as your mentor.

o You can likewise search for someone inside the industry and associated with your company or in the similar line of business. Be that as it may, it's anything but a good plan to approach your immediate rivals.

o The person mentoring you ought to be someone you can appreciate and for whom you have high esteem and respect. The person ought to be exceptionally persuading, and empowering. It is attractive that you two offer some natural qualities like qualities, style of working, and a comical inclination with your mentor.

Having a Meaningful Relationship

o Friendship ought to ideally not be the criteria in a mentor relationship. It ought to find on common respect, trustworthiness, and dependence.

o A mentor's worry ought to fittingly respond with any assistance that he or she may require in something where you may have the capacity to help. Indeed, even a primary card or a little Christmas show goes far to state that you honestly acknowledge what he/she is improving the situation you.

o You ought to always respect the time that your mentor is providing for you. You shouldn't push the person by calling at unforeseen times or being excessively penniless. On the off chance that things can pause, it ought to ideally held until the next gathering.

o Everybody requires different levels of assistance so you can commonly decide on your gathering times, which may happen each other week, once per month, or on an at-require premise.

Having a good mentor can fundamentally support your career prospects and development. So what are you sitting tight for - discover a mentor now!

Why You Need a Career Mentor

Mentors are an essential asset for success at work. Finding one can be an assignment, situating you to be chosen as a mentee is another. Here are some useful hints.

Mentoring used to be a casual and troublesome process. Managers would distinguish potential success stories. You must be affable or someone who helped the mentor to remember his or her initial years. The fairway or a round of billiards would open chances to groomed. Connections would create over cold brews. You got it, the "good old kid" organize.

Companies today understand the hierarchical advantage of supporting and creating ability and are setting up formal mentor programs that guarantee growth from the base to the best proceeds from inside. Will workers remain longer on the off chance that they sense that they are the groom for success? You are the best alternative for another chance if your career guided by the manager, administrator, mentor, or an expert?

Having a mentor enables access to data that may not generally be accessible to you. Mentors give you the general tour, they loan you a hand, and they give understanding into a world that keeps on changing as you explore through it. Mentors provide quality data since more than likely they have committed similar errors you are addressing, so your advantage from the mystery weapon. Consider your colleagues; everybody needs to get advanced all in the meantime. You better accept on the off chance that you have a solid mentor and you are following his or her advice you ought to have an edge.

Motivation-A good mentor has the remarkable capacity to disclose to you what you need to do and why, in a way that makes sense. Experience with a mentor frequently turns into a defining moment in your career or business.

Success-A mentor who imparts their experience to you helps you to stay away from botches that you would some way or another make. Making progress quicker and with less exertion, would you view that as productive and compelling?

Trustworthiness, A mentor, is a man who isn't sincerely engaged with your circumstance, your friends, family, hairdresser, or hairstylist love to give advice. These people either, don't have the foggiest idea, are enthusiastic included, or let you know what you need to here. A mentor's advice ought to be free and straight to the point.

Uplifting Attitude- kicks into your life a good mentor knows you are draining inside, yet they have the arrangement to get you fixed up.

Change Your mentor will expect some make strides. You should expect to develop with information. Mentors will advise homework, for example, books to peruse and courses to take. A mentor may recommend a closet change, perhaps a cleaned look contingent upon your calling.

Career Mentor Can Further Your Career - And How to Find One

A phenomenal career mentor is sufficiently ingenious to shape your predetermination. Finding a good career mentor can be a stroke of good fortunes for a few, while for others, it is the glad finish of a tenacious pursuit.

Helping with a Vocation Right for You

Without a specialist's direction, the more significant part of us winds up in a profession that isn't our true vocation. A job is only a zone of work where we may trudge from morning to night to profit.

Then again, a vocation isn't only a sort of job yet our true calling, which causes us to bring home the bacon as well as gives us incredible bliss and fulfillment. You will begin your working life out of the blue; a career mentor can assist you with the disclosure of your true vocation.

If you have just entered your working life, however, are not encountering a feeling of bliss or inner fulfillment, a good career mentor can enable you to start enjoying your work. Also, they can help you, in the long run, transform your profession into your true vocation.

Helping You from multiple points of view

Distinctive career mentors have one of a kind mentoring programs or individual ways of improving. In any case, what is typical among them is that they all meet with their partners all the time and discuss work-related obliges and troubles.

They can advise you of the most recent changes and advances in that field. They can likewise recommend courses that may support your career prospects, and help you refresh your resume and increase the value of it. Your mentor will enable you to set more up to date and higher objectives, and guide you to accomplish them.

Your Best Career Mentor

On the off chance that you glance around, you will find a lot of career mentors. In any case, the best career mentor is the person who has firsthand experience working in various work areas over some stretch of time. When they have worked in a profession that you are attempting to enter, at that point their recommendation may end up being priceless.

They will admirably share their experiences and viewpoints and help you foresee potential difficulties in that specific field.

Finding a Career Mentor

Numerous colleges run mentoring programs. When you are in the last long stretches of your training, enlist in an application. Likewise, multiple companies and associations additionally have mentorship exercises. There is one in your association, endeavor to exploit it. Be vigilant on an excellent mentor while going to meetings, workshops, and classes. On the off chance that some speaker awes you, don't waver to request that they be your mentor.

If you altogether investigate your own company, you may get pertinent experience. Today, loads of data is openly accessible using your private company's site. Internet networking apparatuses like LinkedIn can give you significant data and help you find a good mentor.

Moving towards administrator you don't straightforwardly answer to is likewise a good thought. You can even search for mentors in other work areas or ventures. They will enable you to expand your perspectives and get things done out of the case.

Finding A Career Mentor

Mentors are critical in any career, regardless of whether you are an understudy in a temporary job, or a full-time worker propelling your career. Did you realize that even company administrators have job mentors? They sometimes pay truckloads of money for their outside mentors, who are genuinely advisors, yet they have them regardless. You ought to have one as well, and you ought to have one for nothing!

Who ought to be your mentor? There are some ways to deal with finding a mentor, and don't hesitate to utilize them both and have numerous mentors.

The first is a specialized mentor, someone who is near your position and can advise you correctly on the most proficient method to enhance your assignment related skills (i.e., how you complete a specific investigation, what exchange magazines you ought to peruse, what are compelling everyday work techniques). This person ought to be someone who is doing exceedingly well at their job, don't search out a mentor who is reliably a low-entertainer!

The second sort of mentor ought to be a career mentor, who ought not to be one of your next line-managers, and most likely ought not to be in your work gathering or association. This person ought to utilize for promoting the more key choices you make in your career (e.g., how would I position myself to land a specific position). He or she ought to be in a place you in the long run need to have (or he/she could have had that position along their career). They ought to be sufficiently learned to disclose to you what longer term things you ought to get required with to get the experience you should obtain that next position you need. At last, they ought to have a good networking Rolodex that they will open up to you when suitable (For instance, in the event that you are keen on position XYZ, and they know someone who deals with that position, they can set up a meeting for you with that person to discuss your enthusiasm for it!).

How would you "enroll" a mentor? A few organizations have techniques effectively spread out, which makes it less demanding. Else, you need to do it all alone.

Networking again has a significant impact in whom you catch wind of and who you meet. Begin with your manager - discuss your more drawn out term career objectives, and let them realize that you need to have an independent mentor or consultant to give you direction along your way. Try to investigate to discover if they know any individual who might fit with your career objectives and would mentor you. More often than not, your manager will be upbeat to try and set up the presentation for you. If your manager can't or won't help, begin making a few inquiries to some coworkers you would trust, and they can most likely do likewise for you.

Next, get that meeting set up, and let them realize that you need their continuous guidance and insight amid your career. Tell your career desires, and mainly where you see them conceivably helping you. You will likewise need to get some information about their experience (to ensure they have the experience to mentor you, and furthermore to ensure the discussion isn't centering around what you need from them!).

On the off chance that that person is certifiably not a good fit for any reason, or it isn't working out amid the procedure, let them know (And clarify why!). Their emotions won't be harm, it's no skin off their back, and it will spare both of you the time and exertion. Merely rehash the procedure to find someone more fitting for the mentor you!

Finding A Mentor At Every Stage Of Career

We get it, finding a mentor can be troublesome and time-devouring. When you do discover one (or two), they can spare you from committing exorbitant errors that can set you back in your career. Having a mentor will enhance the nature of your choices and give openings that won't be accessible to you generally.

There are this thought mentor more seasoned people with built up careers and all around sharpened skill sets who give direction to more young mentees, yet this isn't generally the case. The way to progress is choosing the mentor who best suits your necessities at any given stage of your career: entry level, middle administration level, or executive level. In case you're a business person or innovative person, you can think about these stages as early career, mid-career, and propelled a career.

Interesting points

Despite where you are in your career, it's essential to tolerate at the top of the priority list that there are two parts of working with someone else— essence and form. The core is tied in with sharing heart-to-heart and finding fundamental values. The style is about structure— how you will work together.

Once you've distinguished a potential mentor, meet with them initially to see whether that person is a decent match as far as essence. Do your values adjust? Do your personalities click? Does the discussion stream?

ADVERTISEMENT

If you and your potential mentor have finished the essence test, you can proceed onward to the form part of working together— what you expect to achieve, how you mean to accomplish your primary goal, when you'll impart, and where you'll work together.

Early Or Entry Level

You have as of late begun a job; you can hope to get at work preparing. In case you're fortunate, your new business may have another contract mentoring program. Accept this open door on the off chance that you have it since that person won't just comprehend the essentials of the job. However, they'll be in a decent place to disclose to you how to graph your career path.

Keep in mind that entry level doesn't mean youth. In the present workplace, more people born after WW2 are starting second careers. This pattern was sensationalizing in the 2015 film, "The Intern," where a 70-year-old widower (Robert De Niro), wanting to refresh his skills, acknowledges a job as an intern for an online retailer and turns into the mentee of its 30-something originator and CEO, Jules (Anne Hathaway). The film not just features a high instance of invert mentoring, yet additionally demonstrates how commonly gainful entry-level mentoring can be.

Mid-Career Or Management Level

Once you've settled in and learned the fundamentals of your job, the accentuation will move from specialized skills to people and relationship skills. Your best mentor at this middle stage might be a peer– someone at your same ability and career level– because these people will be comfortable with the sorts of difficulties you confront every day. Keep away from irreconcilable situations; it might be savvy to look for a mentor in a similar field yet work for the other association. This technique upheld by Eileen Carey, the CEO of Glassbreakers, a Tinder-like online platform that matches female item managers, programming engineers, information researchers, and other tech experts with peer mentors.

"We've discovered that peer mentorship was more useful to ladies that we talked with than mentorship from ladies 5 to 10 years above you. People your age comprehend your setting better and can enable you to push ahead."

Executive Or Master Level

You've reached the C suite or have achieved a protected spot at the highest point of your picked calling; it's time to begin considering turning into a mentor. It is an excellent method to experience the reality of the familiar aphorism, "It is smarter to offer than to get." The prizes for going along information and wisdom may not estimate by advancements and expanded profit, but instead, you'll be improving by a profound feeling of reason and euphoria.

Once more, the executive or master stage is characterized more by fitness than age. You've reached this stage when you have great wisdom and experience that can profit others. For instance, you might be a 28-year-old tech master, prepared to mentor middle-matured however less experienced people in your field. The fact of the matter is that you've turned into a pioneer and now it's your swing to develop future pioneers.

Being an executive or master mentor implies that you are a good example, which means you will control your mentee as much by what you do as by what you say. The best senior-level mentors utilize first-rate tuning in and addressing skills, to draw out the worries and goals of their mentees. When you do speak, be authentic. Let your mentee learn from your disappointments, so they don't need to commit similar errors.

As we call attention to in our book One Minute Mentoring, behind even the freest achiever is a person or gathering of people who helped that person succeed. So whether you're in the early, middle, or propelled stage of your career, get into a mentoring relationship. It's a demonstrated path to achieving your objectives, expanding your impact, and finding meaning.

Find the Perfect Mentor for Advance Career

Mentor (n.): a savvy, confided in guide or instructor or robust, senior support or supporter.

A standout amongst the most undervalued and advantageous assets any expert can have amid their career as a mentor. In a regularly becoming focused universe of work, a blend of passionate knowledge, refined, and an extraordinary network will give you the development direction you're going for in your career. If you speak with any proficient (senior) skilled, the last bit of that astound is credited to having a mentor. In your path to progress, it's essential to have direction and real consolation from someone who has let's not go there again.

Here are six techniques for finding a career-characterizing mentor:

Uncover shrouded diamonds in your present network.

Begin with your dearest companions at work who have a comprehension of you professionally and personally. The adage " If you don't ask, you will never get" couldn't be all the more obvious. Try not to be hesitant to put yourself out there and approach your partners for proposals of former coworkers or achieved companions who might be an excellent fit for you (as a mentor). Moreover, connecting with your friends who work in a comparable industry can end up being productive on various fronts. Tell them where you are rationally, and what you are hoping to pick up from a mentor in your corner. When they have recommended a couple of names, set aside the opportunity to do some exploration of your own by investigating their Linkedin and Angellist profiles to improve the feeling of their career direction before you connect.

Keep in mind your (proficient) legacy.

You may not be at your past boss for an assortment of reasons, yet there might be an opportunity you're passing up by disregarding this choice. Recollect a portion of the managers you appreciated speaking with and have shared values. Consider contacting them to connect further (be adaptable; espresso, lunch, quick Skype call) and make up for lost time. At times, managers who worked in a working cross group could be perfect too. Your mentor doesn't need to be in your immediate profession altogether for the relationship to commonly used. Building a relationship with someone who's supposition you trust is established all the more profoundly in them understanding your aspirations and having a solid feeling of authority that can help direct your central leadership at essential emphasis purposes of your career.

Network deliberately.

This mentor obtaining the procedure, albeit compelling, may take more time to emerge because you need to construct the underlying relationship before you can build up a "formalized" mentor relationship. Likewise, not all industry occasions draw in high bore experts that you'll need to connect with, so be essential about which ones you go. On the off chance that you put time into an occasion, ensure you are venturing out of your standard range of familiarity by connecting with new faces and making astute inquiries that start the incredible discussion and help you learn about their experiences. You may discover your mentor in the most startling of spots, so don't rebate anybody before learning more about them.

Try not to ignore your peers.

Contingent upon where you are in your career, it's important to think about partners as mentors. We as a whole have distinctive experiences and learnings given how we got to where we are, so there might learn opportunity for both of you.

Try to learn from contrasts.

Naturally, we are pulled in to what we are most acquainted. When you're hoping to discover a mentor, be available to connect with someone that might not have precisely the same or approach as you. The contrasts between the both of you can at last prompt you learning a great deal more about yourself and the other way around. There isn't only one path that prompts achievement, and it's vital to increase practical learnings and wisdom from various sources. Even though distinctions can add more to the mentor relationship, characteristics, for example, genuineness, honesty, and extraordinary listening skills are an absolute necessity.

Know your value as a mentee.

One of the greatest misguided judgments around mentorship is that you are searching for someone to enable you to accomplish your objectives. A mentor is a dynamic relationship that includes the two sides offering some incentive and feedback to each other. The more experienced people can contribute at another limit however your apparent absence of experience does not bar you. Being more amateur in your field and during the time spent learning about yourself enables you to have less inclination towards standards.

Mentor Who Can Completely Transform Your Career

In the present profoundly competitive business world, having a mentor can mean the distinction amongst progress and disappointment. For anybody seeking proficient development, mentors might be a standout amongst the most significant assets you can take advantage of to provide guidance, advice, bolster, key input, and frequently a new point of view to an issue.

In an ongoing review of 45 CEOs who had mentors, 84% revealed that mentorship relationships helped them maintain a strategic distance from costly oversights and learn insights into their career ways all the more rapidly. Taking care of business, mentors can enable you to open your maximum capacity, collect generally challenging to reach information about your industry or claim to fame, and persevere mishaps without losing center or certainty. Choosing the wrong mentor, then again, can result in an inefficient, baffling relationship that draws you no nearer to accomplishing your career objectives, potentially separating an association. Here are a couple of tips I've gotten throughout the years for finding the right mentor and fashioning a useful, enlightening relationship:

A mentor ought to motivate you to improve

Nobody is flawless, and your initial step to finding a mentor is mindfulness. Be straightforward with yourself, and determine precisely the area(s) you need to improve keeping in mind the end goal to flourish in your expert life. Your mentor ought to be someone who exceeds expectations in these zones, as well as rouses you to do likewise. It is safe to say that you seem to be a more successful communicator? At that point seek out individuals who make you think, "I wish I could convey what needs resemble that amid gatherings." Do you need to build your item management range of abilities? At that point find someone who embodies those capacities in your eyes.

Be clear about what you need—and don't sugarcoat it.

Before you set out on a mentor/mentee relationship, you need to be forthright about your desires. What are your objectives, and for what reason do you figure this individual can enable you to accomplish them? Trustworthiness is critical, particularly at this beginning period. Don't tell your potential mentor what you think he or she needs to hear. Speak your mind, and determine together if this relationship is useful for the two gatherings.

There's such an incredible concept as excessively experienced.

In case you're an ongoing college alumnus merely entering the workforce, it's impossible that a C-suite executive is a right mentor for this phase of your career. Whatever your position, search for someone who can stroll in your shoes, and comprehend or identify with the particular challenges you confront. In the meantime, be watchful about approaching partners who have excessively comparable of a resume. These relationships can without much of a stretch end up focused—a dynamic that advantages neither of you.

Search for someone who shares your energy and issue

While a compelling mentor needs to be eager about you and your career, a standout amongst other approaches to guarantee fervor is constructing the relationship in light of a familiar intrigue. So ask yourself, "What issue am I enthusiastic about understanding?" Maybe it's a challenge confronting your association or industry. Possibly it's a social issue, similar to training. Whatever the problem may be, search for someone who is endeavoring to comprehend it and request to include.

Gain your mentor's regard

From a mentor's perspective, you are a venture—and one that won't settle. If you need the relationship to thrive, you need to win it. It implies stifling your personality when your mentor offers reactions you'd rather not hear and doing your best to assume that individual when his or her advice negates your judgment. You likewise need to regard your mentor's consideration as an essential asset, so make sure to have an arrangement for each gathering. You get the most out of every communication while never sitting around idly.

CHAPTER TWO

A Career Mentor - Help Advance a Career

Numerous people find they are battling with their present place of employment for an assortment of reasons. The absence of motivation and drive expedite it a battle, a career mentor may be the thing for you. You are not precisely beyond any doubt what this sort of mentor is or what they do; they mostly are there to help direct your career motivating.

They are there to give you unprejudiced advice concerning your career. The best mentors are people who are in the same field of business from yourself – that way they can provide better and more taught career advice. Alongside being in a similar area, you additionally need a mentor who is more refined than you.

They will have the capacity to give you sound advice regarding how to advance your career. You can utilize a career mentor both when you have a job and when you are searching for one. When you as of now have the job, they will have the capacity to enable you to do what you need to advance and take your career to the following level. The fact is that it may be advantageous to request that your manager be your mentor, you should fight the temptation. You two usually have distinctive career objectives as a top priority and managers regularly don't have sufficient energy to mentor you. A right decision would be someone higher up in your company or even someone outside the company yet at the same time in the business. Merely make any doubt you don't look for the assistance of an immediate contender.

When you utilize a career mentor to enable you to find a job, they will have the capacity to allow you to plan for interviews, and also investigate your resume. It is not the same as having a job enrollment specialist. You need to recall that it isn't your mentor's job to find a job for you. They are there for when you need advice and need someone to converse.

Make beyond any doubt that the mentor you pick is someone you respect and whose feeling you respect. A mentor if you are not going to hear them out or acknowledge their conclusions and advice.

Utilizing a career mentor may be only the thing you need to get your career to the following level. Even though you probably won't have known about this term previously, it is winding up progressively famous as the feelings of anxiety of having a job expanded. Even though it helps to respect your mentor, it isn't necessitating that he or she is your friend. Having a friend as your mentor may result in one-sided advice.

A mentor is undoubtedly not a shut individual. " A mentor imparts his experiences to you not simply to flaunt his accomplishments, but rather to make you comprehend that there is in every case promising finish to the present course of action." The answer to the question regarding for what reason completes one need a mentor - the answer is somewhat necessary. None of us are equipped for dealing with every one of the complexities of career and also personal growth. Occasions are not uncommon when we remain at the intersection of life and contemplate about which is the right bearing to take for ultimate satisfaction and thriving. A mentor satisfies every one of these requirements, and the sky is the limit from there. Be that as it may, where does find a person with such properties? Ordinarily, you would have discovered a mentor without naming him or her all things considered, as the person exhorts and counsels you in essential matters concerning your career, and so on. It is by chance that you have discovered a mentor without making a decent attempt for it! It could be your associate, unrivaled or even your mate or closest friend. If you are not as fortunate, you could approach us, an expert preparing establishment who could manage you to the right person or a related program, where you could find what you are searching for.

Last yet never the minimum critical part of this dialog is for what reason is it imperative to wind up a mentor? View yourself as favor and bless to have been endowed with the fundamental characteristics of a mentor: open in correspondence, convincing capacities, and sufficient experience in a specific expertise zone and additionally in life when all done, experience is meeting a wide assortment of people and circumstances both in proficient life and that's only the tip of the iceberg. Would it not be pleasant to sharpen your aptitudes additionally? It said that whichever call you are in; there is no end to learning. What better open doors are there in life, which can enable you to build up your insight and experience than mentoring and helping other people accomplish their fantasies? Being an active mentor could imply that you contact people's lives where it matters most.

Mentor to Help Further Your Career

You ought to consider becoming the piece of a mentoring program. Numerous jobs, for example, teaching make the protégé-mentor relationship a compulsory one. Most posts don't reveal all they have to offer on a primary day, month or even year at work. It is the reason a mentor is helpful to you. Orientation at some companies will enable you to work with a mentor. Utilize all the information your mentor offers. You should take advantage of any preparation that your employer gives you too. Having a mentor at your place of employment can be a precious, positive experience.

Make inquiries at professional associations. A mentor can found inside your professional association. Attempt to find people who might consider 'career veterans.' You ought to get a mentor who has the same career as that which you need. You can put a promotion in the paper for a person to chat with to get advice. Numerous people in the same career might help you out with your job.

Ask a friend whom you trust. There might be someone who offers to be your mentor before you see you need one. You ought to be able to find a mentor in a friend or even a relative to help in developing your career. To help you down your career way, make sure that he or she has the same objectives as you. Be sure you are on the same track regarding what you need to get out of the mentor-protégé relationship. Find a kind friend with ethics and a purpose like you have who will mentor you.

Nothing is useful as a mentor in the workplace. They can guarantee your success. Merely seek someone who has the same career description as you do and you'll benefit from developing a mentor-protégé relationship with him or her.

Career Mentorship - Helping You Achieve Job Growth

As far back as we were youthful, we always had our folks, instructors, and different grown-ups to control us. They thought us what is right and what isn't right. They additionally instructed us how to carry on in specific circumstances. These little life exercises were necessary because they were to set us up for life as independents. When we are living alone and have our particular jobs, it very well may be an utterly extraordinary circumstance. Even though you may increase a few companions, you can't give them your trust entirely. When we need to prevail in life, we need to consider ourselves first. In any case, we additionally need someone to go about as a guide when we are in the work setting. When we are doing our best to achieve the top of our career step, we need to have a mentor to provide us direction and proposals that we will have the capacity to make full utilization.

When you find yourself confounded amidst your calling, you can extraordinarily profit by a career mentor. Difficulties are always a piece of life, and you will undoubtedly go over a few of them when you are in the workforce. You don't necessarily need to experience only them since you can always have a dear companion or partner go about as a mentor. Through mentorship, you can even increase a few bits of knowledge and clearness when you find yourself bewildered midway into your calling. These individuals can provide you with valuable reactions. You need to keep a receptive outlook when they are conversing with you since they know better and need the best for you. They won't have the capacity to provide you with much assistance on the off chance that you don't make sure that you tune in to what they need to state.

Additionally, they will have the capacity to provide you direction amidst the most troublesome and befuddling challenges. Regardless of whether you are precisely at the ugly start of your job seek, mentors will have the capacity to find the most reasonable career for your personality and abilities. With their assistance, you can even take advantage of gifts and capabilities you thought you never had. On top of that, you will have the capacity to sharpen your abilities with their assistance.

Remember that a mentor ought to be someone that you have always gazed upward too. These individuals need to have the experience and information that they can use to help you in your life as an expert. Keeping an open relationship with your mentors is exceedingly suggested because you would need to open up to these individuals and disclose to them what you seek to be, and what aptitudes you would need to create. Keep in mind forget that your mentor isn't there to judge you. They are there to lead you into the most reasonable path that will enable you to achieve the career development you need.

The Importance of Career Mentoring

Something that separates successful people from whatever left of us is coaching or mentoring. Shrewd people know they don't have every one of the appropriate responses themselves, as well as other people have conclusively discovered through their own particular experiences the best approach for a specific field.

The majority of the present elite athletics people have coaches. They can be general or pro - wellness, abstain from food, specific abilities and so on. Lawmakers have to talk and composing coaches. Vocalists have voice coaches, performing artists, artists - all in the highly paid games and diversion businesses. The prizes are high if you achieve the best, and there is a scarcely discernible difference amongst success and disappointment.

Career mentoring is the same. You have to get the upper hand over whatever remains of the workforce. It could be expanding your chances of advancement in your current company, or searching for another position somewhere else. You could be considering starting your own business.

How would you start? It isn't keen to re-develop the wheel, so you have to discover someone who has just been down the way and has been successful. They comprehend what works and what doesn't work. They can control you the correct way, and stop you going off on digressions. Ensure the coach is believable. Have they done it without anyone else's help? For what reason would it be advisable for you to hear them out?

You should take a gander at your career so far - where have you been successful? What have you delighted in doing? What are your qualities? It's essential to look at what you should need to do considering, e.g., where you have to live, change among work and family, travel, security, and moreover financial issues. It squanders your time applying for jobs that don't meet your criteria. It wastes your time not taking advantage of your abilities and experience by not showcasing them effectively. It additionally spends your time conveying a vast number of resumes with a minor chance of success.

You should realize that networking is the way to success, and the best way to use your network of family, companions, associates, business partners, church individuals, proficient affiliations and so on. An excellent career coach will empower you to manufacture an active network that will flourish through shared help.

You endeavor to do everything all alone, your chances of success will be the much lower in contrast with someone that utilizes the assistance of a coach or mentor. While the services of a coach are not free, the sum paid is a great venture that will pay for itself many times over later on. You should be clear about what you will get for your money. There are a few organizations out there that charge a colossal sum for faulty advantages - be cautious.

Before you start working with a career coach or mentor, you should be flawlessly clear about what services you will get for your money. Request that the supplier clarify what you get, and the esteem it will bring. Ask the supplier what prove they have that a specific service is active. Have they improved the situation themselves, or would they say they are merely doing a business showing with regards to on you? What is the foundation of the person you are managing? Would you be able to meet with or address the genuine coach/mentor before you join? What is their experience and experience in the field? How could they get their present and past positions?

Do your examination before you submit your well-deserved dollars? While having a quality coach, who has "been there, done that" can have a significant effect, someone of low quality won't just give low an incentive to money, yet also put you off coaching services. We return to the start of this success is a group activity – ensure your group is of a high bore.

3 Tips for Choosing the Right Mentor to Advance Your Career

Career headway is a noteworthy worry in the US. With the American unemployment rates always fluctuating here and there, many are swinging to mentors and career coaches for assistance. In case you're looking for inventive ways for advancing your career, a mentor might be what you need. However, is finding the right mentor for you. It can be very dubious for a few people. That is the reason it's important to know a portion of the keys to finding a career mentor that will be qualifying in helping with advancing your career. Additionally, since this person will coach you, it's essential that your mentor is someone you can personally work with to take care of business. Here are three excellent tips to enable you to pick the right mentor for advancing your career:

1. Find People You Admire

Recognize the type of people you admire and turn upward too. Remember that appreciation and respect don't necessarily go as one. Because you have respect for a person, say your supervisor, doesn't mean you admire them. Your connection may originate from the level of an expert they hold in your life. Be that as it may, genuine adoration goes past respect. It's a profound sentiment of endorsement of that person's qualities.

When you have identified the type of people you genuinely admire, this will set the bar for the kind of mentor you ought to search. You need to find someone who has a liberal soul that appreciates helping people. Ensure they have as of now effectively experienced the career path you're on. They will be more will to impart their encounters to you and help you with advancing your career.

2. Demand a Meeting

You should have an open correspondence with your mentor. Regardless of whether they are a relative, proficient career coach, initiative engineer or an online career administration master, you should meet with them. When you have identified the type of mentor you admire, set up a meeting to become acquainted with them better. On the off chance that they're not willing to speak with you, at that point you know from the get-go in the diversion that they won't have room schedule-wise to coach you at advancing your career.

When you contact your potential mentor, give him a concise clarification regarding why you need his assistance. Give genuine compliments with the goal that he'll know why you've picked. Offer your dreams for what you hope to pick up from their mentoring. It appears as energized as you seem to be, you've discovered an incredible mentor that you can identify. Mentor will be more than willing to assist you with advancing your career.

3. Planning is the Key

Not every person can find a quality mentor. However, if you're one of the fortunate ones, you would prefer not to squander your mentor's time.

Begin Advancing Your Career Today

Whatever approach you decide to take to find the right mentor for you, you should begin towards that goal today. Set some sensible desires with the intention that you won't squander your mentor's time. When you find the perfect career coach, you'll be well on your way to advancing your career.

Why Having A Mentor Is So Important For Your Career
CAREER MENTOR:
Keep in mind when investing in energy with your mentor implied taking counsel from grandpa or figuring out how to peruse with your primary teacher? Since youth is in the back view reflect, who is the person that cows you in the right direction?

Having an expert mentor can provide career understanding in all industry fields, including human services and loft enterprises. It can enable you to gain from someone who has "just been there." He or she can open entryways, offer guidance, and help you through a troublesome circumstance.

3 THINGS TO REMEMBER:

1. It doesn't always happen immediately. Much the same as a most excellent relationship, it requires some dangerous energy.

2. Go to your mentor meetings arranged and catch up with any to-dos.

3. Associate in a way that is snappy and simple for your first meeting. Time is of high incentive to the vast majority.

WHERE DO I FIND A MENTOR?

Joining proficient partners, organizing associations or online industry bunches is an incredible way to distinguish individuals that potentially would be a solid match.

IT FEELS AWKWARD ASKING, "WILL YOU BE MY MENTOR"

While some mentor relationships can naturally characterize, a name isn't always vital. Finding someone who is congenial is useful. Have a go at asking a potential mentor, "Might I be able to get you some espresso sometime in the following couple of weeks? I'm exceptionally inspired by how you wound up effective in what you do." You may be astonished; honeyed words can go far.

Choose a Mentor That Will Do What It Takes to Aid You in Your Success

So you're at long last decided to get involved in the home-based business, and you are not able to do it all alone. Presently understand that there are numerous purported "coaches" yet which one is going to be there for your success?

The principal thing you ought to be aware of is their income. Presently as weird as this sounds, and as odd as it is to ask someone's salary, it is very vital to know this. The fundamental reason being, would you need to be instructed by someone who is making less than you? Presently I can understand on the off chance that it is a motivational speaker and not a die-hard business person, but instead, even still, they should, in any case, have a healthy income.

Complete an intensive search on them by utilizing one of the massive search engines. Get a feel for what they remain for and what their reasoning is. You would be surprised on what soil that you can find on someone. Parts more people whine rather than compliment. What's more, it can likewise work to support them by showing honors or positive book about what they have done.

Keep in consistent contact with them. If need to mentor you, you will return your emails/brings promptly. Before you use them, figure out a reasonable price and see if its possible to pay a month to month statement. Along these lines, it keeps confidence in everyone' s best interest.

Once you have established a steady relationship with them, take the necessary steps to complete your assignments and dependably listen to them. After all, they realize what they are doing. Also, on the off chance that they are making a considerable measure of money, you'd better listen great. Soliciting parts from questions is excellent. Try not to insult your mentor by testing them or questioning them with thoughtful or wry comments. By giving them respect, you are enabling them to open up to you and expand their knowledge to you.

By utilizing your coach/mentor for what they meant for(teaching), ought to will be able to reap the rewards of knowledge which thus will equal benefits. Carefully following directions and executing them promptly with massive activity is your key to success. Get started learning with your mentor today.

CHAPTER THREE

A Mentor Program Makes Great Sense!

A lot of people who enter the workforce without being prepared at all! Indeed, they may have an exceptional instruction. However, they don't have the vital abilities that will enable them to wind up an extremely gainful individual from staff in their company. The extremely incredible thing about a mentor program is exceptionally essential to ingrain the values and goals of the organization into teams or crews that have fantastic potential for development.

A lot of organizations have come to understand the intense speculation that is required to train and to create staffs. With a decent mentoring-program, organizations will fix the tote strings yet will likewise assist employees with being as well as can be expected be. A lot of organization structure include directors or chiefs to give training and create workers who work in the organization, in all actuality they don't ordinarily fill in as mentors.

What a mentor does is to offer advice, targets, and headings to workers that are looking to fabricate and build up their career. Mentor-programs influence employees to feel that they are adding a substantial and essential piece of the company. It will create faithfulness and an excellent drive to be exceptionally useful in each zone of the job.

A lot of workers may genuinely not entirely comprehend the strategies and the structure of the company that they work. Mentors will instruct and train employees on the organization's goals and center values. Mentors will likewise show employees polished skill and the right office manners. It's a well-known fact that a lot of youngsters do not have the compelling artwork of demonstrable ability and will inevitably require some direction around there. A mentor program will unquestionably not cost an arm or leg and is an incredibly incredible way to offer the proficient course. There are sites devoted to showing workers in specific callings the right way to expand their impact, pertinence, and value according to others. You don't need to pay a penny to get top quality advice that will take you to the following level and past!

A mentor is one that has exhibited exceptional accomplishment in their picked field. Great mentors are the ones that can without much of a stretch confer their insight in the best way. These people genuinely appreciate cooperating and educating others. People who have mentors are known to be much more useful than the ones who don't. Organizations are helped by mentors to create and furthermore secure their interest in their staff since it is costly to train and contract staff.

The 3 Career Mentors Everyone Should Have

With regards to work, everyone needs advice. Regardless of whether you don't know how to handle a task or need to talk through an intriguing job offer that left the field, there's nothing superior to having a couple of mentors to enable you to out en route.

Except if your company offers a formal mentorship program, it's not always simple to discover people that way. Who would it be a good idea for you to swing? What's more, more fundamentally, how would you approach them and fabricate relationships with them after some time?

The procedure is somewhat unique for everyone—some mentoring relationships usually happen, while others require additional exertion. In any case, there are three types of mentors that everyone ought to have—and we've assembled a guide on the best way to get them.

Mentor 1: You in One Year

Consider your short career goals: Where would you like to be as of now one year from now? Search for a person who's as of now there, and search her out to be your "where I need to be in a year" mentor. Preferably, this person is someone who's being in your shoes and can without much of a stretch identify with your present encounters.

This type of mentor is incredible when you require advice on the easily overlooked details, similar to the ideal way to approach a task.

You work for a massive organization; you can ordinarily locate this sort of mentor just by mingling and becoming acquainted with people in your office. You work for a little company or office, it very well may be harder, yet don't be reluctant to connect with people in your network or at industry occasions—a great many people are glad to assist!

Begin the relationship by taking her out to espresso and getting some information about her present place of employment, how she got to where she is, and if she has any advice for you. From that point onward, keep it easygoing: Hopefully, you'll be sufficiently agreeable to connect with her again as inquiries or issues come up.

Mentor 2: Your Five-Year Guide

While a one-year mentor is extraordinary for the everyday stuff, it's likewise great to have a "where I need to be in five years" mentor. With more experience added to her repertoire, this person can offer you advice on progressing inside your company or field, including the transient goals you ought to set keeping in mind the end goal to arrive.

When you're searching out this person, take a gander at mid-to senior-level chiefs who are outstanding and regarded inside your company. If you have thought of someone who's in your fantasy part, however, don't have any acquaintance with her personally, discover an associate who does and request a presentation, or checks whether you would all be able to snatch lunch or beverages after work.

From that point onward, however, keep your relationship with this mentor more fastened. Approach her for a gathering or espresso, and treat it relatively like an instructive meeting. Have a few inquiries prepared to get some information about her career path and how she got to where she is currently. At that point, check whether she'd meet with you each quarter or so to talk about your career path. In particular, keep things expert, and ensure you don't bring office dramatization in with the general mishmash. Hello, she may wind up being your manager one day!

Mentor 3: Your Career Planner

This type of mentor may take more time to discover and will probably change all through your career. This relationship will likewise most likely develop naturally—when you're the first beginning, it might be your most loved teacher from school, or, later not far off, it might be a previous partner or manager. You can have more than one of these types of mentors, as well—it never damages to have a couple of incredible personalities in your group.

While it's great to check in with this mentor consistently, it's most vital to counsel her amid times of progress. Offer with her your goals, request her assistance in making sense of how to arrive, and look for her advice on any significant advances you're thinking about, such as going to graduate school or tolerating another position.

All through your career, there will be lots of people you swing too for help and advice. In any case, by being crucial and recognizing a couple of critical mentors to be your "leading body of guides," you'll ensure that advice is always controlling you in the right course.

Step by step instructions to Find a Career Mentor

Good career mentor intentionally gives that career advice and help. The relationship you'll have with your mentor will be progressing, and your mentor can guide you for the duration of the life of your career. It's a relationship that can keep going quite a while. A mentor can be essential both when you're starting out and when you're climbing the career stepping stool.

Who and How to Ask for Help

Maybe the most significant advance in seeking after a dream job is to find someone who as of now works in that field who can offer guidance and advice as you continue. I realize that sounds threatening. However, it doesn't need to be. Trust it or not, this isn't as troublesome as it may seem.

In my experience, numerous people express dread at the possibility of requesting assistance from a prospective mentor who is an aggregate stranger. For what reason would they need to encourage you? The answer is simple: people like helping other people!

By approaching a prospective mentor for help, you're telling them they appreciate for what they do and that their career sought after. It's a good inclination, and numerous people need to know their experiences and bits of knowledge are significant to others.

It's not widespread, apparently, and not every person will see it like this. You may keep running into a person who thinks maybe a mentorship candidate who couldn't care less what people think and isn't interested in helping you along your career path. In any case, you'll see, once you start asking, you'll be amazed at exactly how open numerous people are.

Not all mentor candidates will be strangers. You may have a previous manager, educator, or your relatives or friends may know about someone who might have the capacity to encourage you.

Tips for Finding a Good Career Mentor

Indeed, even with a couple of uplifting statements, searching for and finding a career mentor may appear to be unnerving, so here are a couple of tips to you kick you off:

You're fresh out of the plastic new or evolving careers; it might be a good plan to explore the field and find out about the best people who are in it.

Realize what you can about their experience, training, and even regular interests.

Make a rundown of people who appear as though they may be good fits for you and your career goals.

Start contacting the people on your rundown yet run gradually with everyone. Start with a polite and formal email to present yourself and see who responds.

Be tolerant – your potential mentor candidates might be occupied, and it could take a multi-day or two for any of them to respond.

Endeavor to frame a relationship with them and become more acquainted with their personalities even as you attempt to show yours. As such a large number of different things, when you find the correct mentor, you'll know it.

The guidance and advice from a good career mentor might be what you need to guide you through your next set of career steps. Good fortunes and who knows? Perhaps some time or another someone will contact you to be their mentor.

A mentor is someone who consents to share their attitudes, information, ability, and expert contacts with you. Mentors can enable you to set career goals, resolve troublesome issues, and settle on sound career choices. People with mentors procure higher compensations, are advanced all the more every now and again and report higher job fulfillment than those without mentors. Sounds good, isn't that so? You may as of now have one, since many mentoring relationships emerge naturally at work or in school. Be that as it may, if you've wound up without a mentor, and you need one, here's the way to approach finding one:

1. What do you need from a mentor?

As a matter of first importance, you're searching for someone who's interested in mentoring. Other than that essential, it's dependent upon you to recognize what sort of person you're seeking. Here are a few inquiries to consider:

> Are you searching for someone nearby? Is it necessary for you to meet in person?

It is safe to say that you are searching for someone with a specific skill set? Or then again who works in a particular field?

> What sort of time duty would you say you are searching?

What's important to you regarding personality? For instance, might you want to be mentored by someone who is active and disorderly, or quiet and calm?

What would you like to pick up from the relationship? For instance, do you need guidance on a particular undertaking or would you be able to utilize continuous help influencing a career to change?

2. Would it be advisable for you to search for a mentor?

When you limit what you need from a mentor, searching for one turns into somewhat less demanding. Here are a couple of places to look:

Inside your network: Former chiefs, educators, volunteer directors, or contacts you know through your friends and family are extraordinary places to start. Furthermore, keep in mind your weak ties.

Strangers: Perhaps nobody in your quick network very fits what you're searching. There is no mischief in viewing a stranger as your mentor, and there are a couple of places to look:

Look for potential mentors web-based utilizing LinkedIn.

Glance through the individuals from associations identified with your field or the field you're interested.

Check the graduated class index of your place of graduation for potential associations.

Programs: There are a developing number of programs that encourage mentoring relationships. Numerous fellowship programs –, for example, the Fellowship for Emerging Leaders in Public Service – interface members to mentors. Net Impact has a Career Connections program that enables business experts to achieve each other on the web. Start by investigating participation associations in your field and network, for example, the Young Nonprofit Professionals Network, Emerging Practitioners in Philanthropy, and Association of Fundraising Professionals.

Additionally, it might appear to be natural that you'll need a mentor from your expert field, however, don't rebate the estimation of a mentor from an altogether different calling or foundation. Mentoring relationships can traverse numerous years, so your mentor may finish you a few job changes.

3. What does your relationship resemble?

In your underlying contact, send an email approaching to get together for espresso, in their office, or a telephone call. Lead this underlying gathering like an educational meeting: make some particular inquiries about their career path and experiences. Likewise, get a sense of the science. It is an exploratory discussion to get a sense of regardless of whether you'll be an incredible match.

If the person is eased back to respond or gives vague answers, maybe it is anything but a good time for them to be a mentor. Try not to think about it literally!

Once you've built up contact with the person, keep on cultivating the relationship. Keep in mind, networking is a two-way road, so if you can give valuable data to your potential mentor, do it! Now, you're likewise trying things out yourself — is this person who you need to be your mentor? Is it true that you are clicking?

If it is yes, you might need to formalize the relationship. One methodology may be to inquire as to whether you can set up a customary month to month meeting to check in. At last, the structure of the relationship is dependent upon you and your mentor.

Need a Good Mentor? Here's How to Find One

Exploring your career and making sense of how to excel can be overwhelming, particularly in case you're endeavoring to go only it. Regardless of how autonomous you are, you'll get where you need to run quicker with a little help — and that assistance can come as a mentor.

In investigate from Accountemps staffing firm, 86 percent of executives said having a mentor is vital for career advancement — but, just about a fourth of them said they had someone they consistently swing too for advice and guidance. It could be on account of numerous experts don't step up with regards to request mentorship.

"Not very many individuals tend to seek out mentors in the work environment." "Exceed Your Space at Work: How to Thrive at Work and Build a Successful Career." "This is a major miss since mentors are directors, leaders or fruitful associates in the association who know how to succeed."

In any case, corporate workers aren't the main ones who need mentorship. Entrepreneurs can likewise profit by the insights of a confided in the source, maybe considerably more so than can different experts.

"Mentors can be a standout amongst the greatest weapons for an entrepreneur, by giving guidance, astuteness, and connections," an American Express OPEN adviser on government contracting and a mentor for the Open Mentorship Institute program. "Each entrepreneur ought to have a mentor for acquiring the best solutions to his or her day by day challenges amid startup and management."

Even though framing a mentor-mentee relationship must be a shared procedure, there are some key components to remember as you're seeking a mentor. Mentoring and career specialists offered their responses to questions entrepreneurs may have about choosing a mentor who's right for them. [Perfecting Your Mentoring Relationship]

What does a mentor do?

Regardless of whether you're the organizer of a shiny new startup or an entrepreneur with a touch of business encounter added to your repertoire, you can merely profit by having a mentor.

"A mentor can fill in as a sounding board at critical focuses all through your career," executive chief of staffing firm The Creative Group. "They can provide guidance on career management you will most likely be unable to get from different sources and an insider's point of view on the business, and additionally make acquaintances with scratch industry contacts."

Open Mentorship Institute mentor and American Express OPEN adviser on obtainment noticed that mentors could help their mentees recognize and keep away from business traps, and work through the challenges in front of them. Martin-Rosa included that a mentor can likewise spare entrepreneurs significant time and cash by helping them make a guide to progress.

What characteristics does a good mentor have?

And no more fundamental level, your mentor ought to have encounter more noteworthy than your own particular and a reputation of accomplishment in what he or she does. There are a lot of different characteristics the individual who is managing your business choices ought to have. Doug White, the career master, and supervisor of career and management insights site TCG Blog prompted seeking a mentor who has a solid character and characteristics that merit imitating.

"Search for mentors who are bona fide, sympathetic, inventive and genuine," White revealed to Business News Daily. "You need someone who's minding and put resources into your expert development, yet also someone who will speak truth to you. Sometimes you need some valuable feedback or a rude awakening, while different times you need a high five or congratulatory gesture. A well-picked mentor can provide those things."

A mentor in the same business territory from yours might have the capacity to all the more likely comprehend your business' challenges and concerns, yet Story noticed that productive mentoring relationships don't need to occur inside a similar industry. Leadership theory might be more critical.

"Make beyond any doubt that the mentor shares a comparable esteem framework in leadership and management." "Knowing your identity as a pioneer is critical before going into a mentoring relationship. Would you be able to adjust yourself to the right guide?"

A good mentor will speak up for you at tables where you don't pull up a chair — HR, the executive board, and so forth — because this is the place the majority of the choices about your career.

How would you find one?

When you're searching for a mentor, begin by contemplating your career way and narrowing down a couple of leaders who have your fantasy employment, or whom you respect, an area president for Accountemps.

"Effective mentoring relationships happen when the mentor and mentee are the right matches." "Contact someone you think you are alright with, who can be a nonpartisan sounding board, and [who] will likewise provide extraordinary advice."

It is conceivable that your ideal adviser could find you by shot and offer his or her mentorship, yet being proactive in your scan for your mentor (or mentors) is the best approach.

"Attempt to meet the greatest number of experienced experts as you can," she disclosed to Business News Daily. Once you've distinguished someone, "approach your potential mentor and the underlying gathering as you would a meeting. Be set up to disclose what you would like to gain from the individual and why you esteem his or her insights and aptitude, and also what you convey to the table. Don't mess with this stage — you're laying the preparation for a relationship that will ideally endure forever."

5 Questions to Ask Before Choosing a Mentor

Pairing with the wrong mentor can set you back both personally and professionally, so it's essential to require investment to assess your potential mentor before choosing.

Regard of where you are on your entrepreneurial voyage, you can always profit by having a mentor. Mentors can enable you to recognize and keep away from business entanglements and work your way through the challenges you'll experience on your voyage. Learning from mentors will allow you to gain from their slip-ups and abstain from conferring similar ones. In any case, choosing the right mentor is basic.

Pairing with the wrong mentor can set you back both personally and professionally, so it's essential to require investment to assess your potential mentor before choosing. Here are five inquiries to consider before choosing and setting your trust in anyone professing to be an expert or a mentor:

1. Do they have relevant experience?

You'll discover an overabundance of self-broadcasted experts in each side of the web. A portion of those is well-perfused and articulate, influencing them to appear at first glance like they're loaded with intelligence to share. Your mentor ought to have a track record of achievement in what they do. While you can't anticipate that them will spoon-feed all of you the answers, they ought to in any event have relevant experience to enable you to overcome the challenges you may experience.

Besides experience, you ought to likewise search for some essential personal characteristics in your mentors. For example, you need to make beyond any doubt that you both share similar values in the enterprise. There are regularly multiple conceivable goals for each challenge. Pick a person who can comprehend your business challenges and help you overcome them in a manner that merges with your values and style.

2. Have they prevailing on multiple projects, or would they say they are a one-hit wonder?

Be careful with the one-hit wonder who by one means or another prevailing in business by being in the right place at the right time. Because someone has succeeded once doesn't mean they know anything about staying aware of market patterns and grasping appropriate changes to their technique to remain on top of things.

People who have to prevail in multiple projects are the individuals who are centered around their objectives and are deliberate. They focus on changes and grasp them. They know how to alleviate chance and make due over the long haul by soldiering through a wide assortment of economic situations.

3. Is it safe to say you are trying to do you tell others should do?

The ideal way to separate a genuine expert from false prophets is to take a gander at whether they're strolling the discussion. You ought to always tune in to the individuals who have been there instead of wannabe experts who don't try to do they say others should do.

"Experience is the hardest sort of instructor. It gives you the test first, and the lessons come after." Make beyond any doubt that the mentor you're choosing has robust and genuine experience. If your mentor isn't in the trenches that they've been lecturing about, they're passing up some valuable learning experience and have none to grant to you.

4. Does the business display rotate around teaching you to be successful?

In my experience, the best mentors/mentors you can get are the ones who don't effectively offer their time or administrations. Regularly, successful people are seen down in the passage, digging gold for themselves. They don't pitch scoops to gold diggers. With regards to choosing a mentor, I'd instead pick the ones who have demonstrated a track record and who walk the discussion than the individuals who discovered achievement just by teaching others how to be successful.

5. Will we consent to mentor you?

The opposite thing you ought to consider is whether they would be keen on mentoring you. Once you've identified someone you think would be an ideal mentor for you, don't hesitate to contact them decisively. You might be astonished that a great deal of them are congenial via web-based networking media. You can meet them in-person at meetings or even book a call with them through an administration like Clarity.

Disclose to them why you've identified them as a mentor and what you're anticipating from the mentorship, and inquire as to whether they're available to talking about it more. Mentoring is a reality check. You don't need to take after the entirety of their recommendation indiscriminately, yet they indeed enable you to make educated choices. The ideal way to search for a mentor is by narrowing down a couple of pioneers you as of now appreciate. Before choosing a mentor, play out your due tirelessness by asking the above-recorded inquiries to guarantee that they're the ideal match to your needs.

Strategies for Choosing a Mentor for Motivation, Inspiration, and Success

Mentors aren't only for students considered in danger - or for business people at risk of disappointment. Indeed, a quality mentoring relationship is essential to any student, regardless of whether the student occupied with scholastics, another business or needs to center around the company of a significant life. Mentors can help students of numerous kinds set goals and imagine them, and give inspiration and guidance. Mentors can likewise enable students to perceive misfortunes, beat them, and provide shrubs for dominance and accomplishment.

Mentors can likewise facilitate the vulnerability of progress - a period of newest learning endeavors, regardless of whether it's returning to class, taking in another exchange or growing new personal abilities and orders. Also, since most new efforts mean new people, tasks, rehearses and new goals- - even another lifestyle- - it's anything but painful to feel overpowered, particularly when endeavoring to go only it. With the help and friendship of a mentor, changes are smoother. Likewise, endeavors turn out to be increasingly sure.

School, alongside independent business and learning, wanders, for the most part, give a set structure of goals, systems, best practices and even due dates. In any case, without inspiration, motivation, and guidance, a student's goals can go hidden. Over and over again, the student is confused concerning why. A significant relationship with a mentor can change that, and upgrade alternatives and open doors for academic, business and personal development - self-improvement for genuine success.

Choosing a Mentor

Think about the Chinese adage: 'When the student prepared, the educator will show up.' So it just bodes well that the student should first realize what she is searching for in a

Mentor. Settling on the correct decision is vital to acknowledging inspiration, support, and guidance from a mentor and the mentoring relationship. That is the place visualization becomes possibly the most critical factor.

Visualization may sound odd. However, it's something people continuously do. In the case of conveying a virtual valedictorian deliver to a graduating class, crossing the end zone before an uproarious group or scoring high on a critical mid-term or prospective employee meet-up, our psyches are continually at work, playing out our desires. We picture our test grades, the kinds of customers that will develop our vocations and businesses toward the path we predict. Likewise, we photograph our colleagues and companions - the people who share our values and goals. Visualization is a significant determiner of success, so imagine the mentor you envision - and picture a flawless fit!

When you imagine a mentoring genie, consider what impacts, values and traits they'll have that will be critical to your goals.

A "Demonstrated Formula to Create the Life You Desire," mentors assume a critical part in helping people achieve their goals. "The activity of a mentor is to become friends with, test, manage and acclaim - giving confirmation in times of success and inspiration when success appears to be far away."

"The best goals are lined up with one's values, and the best mentor is somebody who shares these values," And it helps if the mentor has finished goals like the students. Therefore, the mentor turns into an excellent example embodied - a guide with insight, firsthand information, and aptitude.

So how does a student approach choose a mentor? Five techniques that demonstrate to affect the most significant mentor-mentee relationship positively:

1. Personal is Paramount: Respect in the eye of the student. Furthermore, respect is personal. Don't depend on other people's assessments of an individual's significance or worth. Pick a mentor whose life way, achievements and method for identifying with people personally rouse you and inspires you. Pick a mentor that you respect because the mentor respects the goals you envision and the values you respect.

2. The mentor will have a handle and accomplish goals that are parallel to the students. The student will profit by the mentor's astuteness and experience, particularly with regards to defining goals and creating action steps. More than likely, a more established mentor will besides have no enthusiasm for the undesirable mentor-mentee rivalry.

3. Trust is a Treasure: In root, the word trust implies faithful. A faithful confided in mentor suggests you can depend on his or her character, capacity, truth and quality. You can talk genuinely to a told in mentor, and they'll share their real to life points of view and facts with you. They give attestation as opposed to disparaging your desire. They provide guidance instead of getting a kick out of your difficulties and misfortunes. Also, the most faithful reliable mentors usually are ready to share their systems with you. Since a trustworthy, dependable mentor has this sort of boldness, as well.

4. Affirm the Commitment: A mentoring relationship will work if the mentor wants to focus on you, and the time to go through with you, regardless of whether just for a couple of hours a multi-month. Likewise, understand that you're additionally focusing on the mentor, and the remuneration he or she will prize is your equivalent commitment, as well.

5. Numerous Mentors May Maximize Results: For most students, a one-estimate fits-all mentor is impossible. Somebody who gives inspiration in scholastics likely won't be the best individual to direct you into the field of sports. Or on the other hand, a mentor who has exceeded expectations in business or as a business visionary may not be the best decision for mentoring your goals as a parent. Choosing two or even three mentors can be an exceptionally shrewd move. More than five will most likely obstruct advancement and success, and make it harder to respect your commitment as a 'student.'

For what reason Should You Choose A Mentor?

When attempting to build up an online business, it is essential that you pick a mentor. A mentor resembles a coach that guides you on the dos and don ts in beginning an online store on the internet. Despite how sure you are in your capacities having a mentor will improve your viability and will help you in getting prompt outcomes in your business. A mentor will spare you time and help you to stay away from a portion of the common mistake made in beginning an online store.

You can stand to employ a mentor or coach that would be perfect to snappy begin your business and stay away from a portion of the common mistake made by a Newbie yet if you can't bear to procure one than find a company or a man and take after their diagram for success. In the fact that at all conceivable, tail one that uses a similar marketing strategy that you choose to utilize or one that can educate you on a good marketing strategy. Most organizations have items that they create to teach you on the unique marketing strategy, and sometimes these courses are incorporated into the essential participation or may require a redesign. In any occasion, it would be further bolstering your good fortune to buy and actualize the methodologies educated in their course to get propelled preparing in executing a marketing strategy that you are happy with utilizing.

The ideal approach to be successful in internet marketing is to find a man or a company that has just made progress and copy what they are doing. You can do it along however it will take any longer to accomplish a specific level of success, and the expectation to absorb information is exceptionally steep, so why endeavor to figure every one of the complexities of this business out yourself. The guide to success has just made sense. The recipe has been spread out, and you should only make a move and take after the outline.

The first decision that you need to make is, who do you take after or who do you be you mentor or what company do you relate with. You must be cautious about this decision because the wrong picked could be hindering to your advance. In internet marketing just like some other everyday issue, you find large amounts of trickery and deceitfulness. The principal reason most advertisers are endeavoring to accomplish is to persuade you is to haul out your MasterCard and buy what they are offering. There are organizations and individual in this industry that are attempting to counterfeit it until the point that they influence it, and them to ask on inexperienced fledglings merely entering the market that not educated, gullible or only don't know any better. The articulation " CAVEAT EMPTOR" purchaser be careful ought to be your prime center when making your picked. So do your due steadiness and pick an individual of a company with a demonstrated reputation for success.

CHAPTER FOUR

Three Fundamental Mistakes To Avoid When Choosing A Mentor

You have chosen a business to join. Great! Presently you need to find the right mentor. There are various personalities out there. You need to find someone who you can get alongside and feel comfortable working.

There are numerous traps people fall into when choosing their mentor. Three specific areas are requiring particular attention.

1) The first, and presumably the most important mistake people make isn't reaching their potential mentor. Numerous people join a business without even sending an e-mail or getting the phone and speaking to the person they will be working.

Try not to make that mistake. It is your business, and you need to be sure that your mentor will be easily accessible. If you call her/him and she/he doesn't answer his phone or return your bring in an incite mold - for the most part inside 24-48 hours - by what means will you be able to rely on him for help when you need it?

The same advice applies to e-mail correspondence. You don't get a personal e-mail response inside 24 to 48 hours when you send an e-mail requesting more information, then that is usually an indication of a heartless mentor.

Remember that the mentor is supposed to be there for you. It will be your business, and you need to make sure that your mentor will help you when you need it most. Having a connection or bond with that person will help in your quest for success. It is substantially more comfortable to work with someone you get alongside and like!

2) The second mistake to avoid when choosing your mentor isn't making enough inquiries. Ask the highest number of questions as you can about the business Find out what specific help can offer you.

Enquire about resources approaches, for example, other team members in his gathering, or leaders in the business, who can help you as well. The more help available, the better.

Find out about your mentor's business foundation. What has she/he done before?

3) The mistake to avoid when choosing a mentor is hurrying your decision. You would prefer not to hop in with the two feet the first time you see a business opportunity. Make entirely sure this is the thing that you need.

Building your business will take considerable time and effort. There are no enchantment bullets or secrets that will make you productive. Try not to feel awful about flame broiling your future mentor. Remember, this isn't personal. It's a business. You have to pay particular mind to yourself. That is YOU!

Choosing a mentor who suits you is the essential initial step to success. Get that right, and you will reap considerable dividends. You will stick in an unfortunate situation on the off chance that you get it off-base.

Mentors and Coaches: How to Find a Great Mentor

A career coach or mentor is a person who can guide you with the benefit of their experience. He or she might be someone more senior from inside your association or someone external to your association who has been successful in the field or abilities you need to develop. Right mentor can help you accelerate career, support your self-development and improve your working relationships. Also, remember that a mentor isn't just helpful in your job the benefits of having a mentor are relevant to all areas of your life - whether fitness, money related or lifestyle.

Decide what area you need help. Examine your life and determine whether you need help with your career, your health or your relationships. When you know the area or areas you need to center around you can begin searching for a suitable mentor.

Who are the best performers? Whichever area of your life you decide to seek a mentor for, find out who the experts are, who does it better than anyone else?

Where's the hangout? Next, find out where your role models hang out - check out networking events and gatherings, industry events and conferences - make a note of anyone who emerges and has the 'presence' you are searching.

Investigate programs. Numerous associations presently have internal mentoring programs that you can become a piece.

When you find the right person you believe to be a suitable mentor, take some time watching them in real life. Make an inquiry or two to find out what other people's conclusion of your chosen mentor is and find out everything you can about their achievements, beliefs, values, and method of operating. It will give you understanding into them before you approach them about mentoring you.

Approach your mentor. Phone your prospective mentor and request to make an appointment to see them. Tell him or her why you need to meet and schedule a time. It is essential that your interactions are professional and show respect for your prospective mentors' time. It demonstrates you are committed to making the best choice.

Have an agenda. When you do meet, have an outline of what you might want to examine. Your plan ought to include why you need to mentor you, for to what extent and what you hope to pick up amid that time. On the off chance that they do agree to mentor you, you would then be able to work out how you can bolster them as well - this ought to be a two-way process.

Agree. If you both decide to proceed, set up an agreement with guidelines about how your relationship will function and what you both expect from each other.

4 Secrets to Finding a Mentor Who's Perfect for You

Searching for a mentor? You're not the only one. The majority of us need to know the key to building a relationship with someone who can prompt our career path, answer us at work questions, and perhaps enable us to arrive the following enormous thing.

In case you're attempting to find "the one," we have the fix for you. Experts from all kinds of different backgrounds shared tales about their mentee-mentor relationships, and what you should search for in yours.

Here are a couple of our most loved goodies.

1. Your Mentor Should Have a Career Path You Want to Follow My advice for finding the perfect mentor is to find someone you need to resemble. You won't progress toward becoming them precisely, yet it will enable you to take the activities essential to get where you need in your specific life's path.

"The best mentors will let you know not to be a duplicate of themselves. Rather, they'll disclose how they got to where they are. Preferably, what you'll learn isn't to do precisely what they did, however, to achieve the comparable turning points by concentrating without anyone else qualities and shortcomings."

2. Your Mentor Should Have Flaws

"Prepare to be blown away. Nor am I. Also, that is the thing that makes our relationship genuine. You don't need to be perfect to be a great mentor. You can be precisely yourself, your identity. You don't need to sit tight for the minute where you sense that you have the most to offer. "

Everybody has imperfections. You ought to expect that your mentor will have a few, as well. Rather than concentrating your endeavors on finding the perfect person to direct you through your career, comprehend that while nobody has an immaculate reputation, everyone has something to offer.

3. Your Mentor Should Help You—and Not Just Flatter You

'Mentors aren't there to flatter you; they're there to encourage you.'"

4. Your Mentor Shouldn't Be Your Only Mentor

"Stop the 'will you be my mentor?' Messages and start being available to grasp the learning openings surrounding you. Ask your partners and executive team members for their perspectives. Look for advice from your immediate pioneer or pioneer once expelled."

There are such a large number of great people out there with a vast amount of exercises to instruct. Rather than endeavoring to find a solitary all-knowing person, assemble a multitude of supporters who can get you where you need to go.

Finding Great Career Mentors

Finding career mentors isn't in every case simple and asking someone you don't know to be your mentor can be intimidating. Get great mentors and defeat the 'finding a mentor nerves' by following these four tips:

1. Illuminate what you need. Before searching out mentors, record your particular expectations and the part you need mentors to play in your career. Do you need someone who can help you slow down systems administration endeavors, help you in learning more about a specific industry or give direction on the most proficient method to be an effective business visionary? Clearing up your expectations, goals, and targets will guarantee you find the right mentors and that the relationships advantage your expert goals.

2. Think outside your workspace and don't confine yourself. Great mentors can be found in an assortment of spots, so spend time looking outside your present working environment. Search out mentors at business and ladies' relationship in your general vicinity, non-benefit associations, church gatherings, local gatherings, for example, business councils of trade, and even inside your family. Numerous people don't understand great mentors can frequently be found inside their family tree!

3. Set up a meeting. Once you've distinguished a potential mentor, request to meet and talk about a conceivable mentoring relationship. Requesting mentoring is a vital advance to make certain you're both clear on the terms. This meeting should happen someplace that is commonly agreeable and where you can talk with certainty.

4. Be clear with your mentor. When you find a person who consents to be your mentor, as a matter of first importance, make beyond any doubt you share a similar promise to your expectations. Be sure about the time required and the accessibility of your mentor, and set up a standard meeting plan with points for exchange and to monitor the goals you've set for yourself.

While getting mentors can be intimidating after these four tips enable you to defeat a severe case of nerves and find specialists that best help your career goals. Also, don't be debilitated if a potential mentor turns you down. Instead, effortlessly express gratitude toward them for meeting with you and attempt to comprehend why - if they're excessively over-burden with work now, perhaps they can mentor you later on. Likewise, inquire as to whether they may recommend someone else. because finding a great mentor might be just a single discussion away!

The Value of Having a Professional Mentor

A stable mentoring relationship based on coordinated effort and the promise to the professional development of either of its participants. While in the normal mentoring relationship, one participant has more experience, skill, knowledge than the other, numerous stable mentoring relationships give an opportunity to the two parties to gain from each other through the development of a minding and aware association.

The Growth of Mentoring in the Social Sector

Corporate mentoring programs have long perceived as a fundamental methodology for drawing in, creating, and holding top representatives. As per an overview by the American Society for Training and Development, 75% of private sector officials said that mentoring had been essential in helping them achieve their present position. In the social sector, worker mentoring programs are more bizarre. While some imaginative organizations are finding a way to make viable interior plans, different organizations offer external programs that interface mentors and mentees; these programs can be an incredible alternative for charities that do not have the resources to give inside programs.

For instance, the Center for Nonprofit Development and the International Mentoring Network Organization have built up their particular mentor-coordinating programs to help associate prepared philanthropic professionals with professionals before their careers. The Center for Nonprofit Development centers around interfacing new however abnormal state not-for-profit leaders with other, more experienced charitable leaders to help them deliberately understand organizational difficulties or make painstakingly created plans for the eventual fate of the mentee's organization. The International Mentoring Network Organization applies an "open source" way to deal with mentoring, giving its individuals access to interviews with experienced professionals, discourse discussions, and a mentor coordinate administration.

Why a Mentor?

There are some benefits to building a mentor relationship with a prepared charitable professional, most outstandingly access to new contacts, knowledge, and skills.

"Mentors can complete some things for your vocation. They can enable you to build your resume, control you on an undertaking, and help you recognize resources, including alluding you to different mentors and critical people in your field.

Mentors furnish creating not-for-profit leaders with the support they probably won't approach generally. For instance, access to the mentor's close to the home network can allow rising leaders to meet imperative people at a significant time in their careers and can widen their scope of conceivable professional chances.

The New Voices National Fellowship Program, directed by the Academy for Educational Development, works on leadership development for human rights activists, as of now concentrating on rising leaders in the Gulf Coast district. New Voices requires every individual taking an interest to have a mentor due to the benefits the organization has seen from these relationships.

"In our program, we've seen mentors help build up the Fellows' vital reasoning, associations and contacts, and resources and openings. Having a mentor furnishes people with an open space in which to raise issues, handling difficulties, and sustain growth."

A mentor is somebody who's knowledge and experience the mentee regards and somebody who's astuteness and know in what manner can support the professional growth and development of the mentee. Frequently this is a supervisor, educator or another philanthropic leader who the mentee has just met, yet now and again a mentor can be somebody who isn't known to the mentee. Mentors don't really should be the most senior individual at an organization or inside the field; the correct mentor relies upon what knowledge the mentee plans to pick up.

"You don't have an idea concerning who to demand to be your mentor, find organizations that work and looking for their leaders. Asking to achieve something as direct as getting a coffee together can be outstandingly productive." Another great technique to attract a mentor is to work together on a wonder that is critical to the two parties. "Pick something that supports your potential mentor's work and demand some help collecting it. "Along these lines, you are both placed resources into completing a target together that can provoke a more significant relationship in the midst of the system."

Maintaining Healthy Mentor Relationships

To make the more significant part of a mentoring relationship, begin with a formal understanding that layouts the parts and desires of the two participants. Counting subtle elements, for example, when the match will meet, how often and for to what extent, and what the objectives of the relationship are will build a solid establishment for the connection. While the span and recurrence of mentoring gatherings differ, most mentoring accomplices meet or talk once every week for around 60 minutes. The configuration and substance of these discussions may fluctuate, however commonly comprise of meetings to generate new ideas to take care of issues, refreshes and subsequent meet-ups on current tasks or more engaged discourse of professional development points. A mentoring relationship ought not to view as an inside track to the best or an opportunity to gripe; it is a conscious and professional relationship in which the two parties can gain from the experience and each other. As the ties create, mentees should remember to impart their triumphs to their mentors and make beyond any doubt the mentor knows how significant their opportunity and knowledge is.

Simple Choosing the Right Career

In today's undeniably focused business condition, numerous people find it amazingly hard to land their optimal positions. Accordingly, an ever increasing number of people wind up jobless, and they have no course throughout everyday life.

Genuinely, an uplifting state of mind assumes a vital part of career determination. We need to make proactive strides when we are looking for circumstances in the job showcase. Share with you four essential tips which can help you to pick the right career for yourself.

1: Ask yourself honestly what you are interested in

Don't just attend interviews you don't know which line you are interested in. "Self-talk" is imperative here. You need to ask yourself whether you jump at the chance to do certain assignments consistently. You are content with what you are doing? When you are "constrained" to accomplish something which you don't care for, regardless of how appealing the compensation bundle is, you will remain long in the field. So for what reason don't you change your career path promptly? Try not to sit idle on things which you have no interest in doing them.

2: Find out whether you have the skills and knowledge for the specific career

There are particular jobs which look extraordinary however with a particular end goal to get utilized; you need to have skills and knowledge. On the off chance that you don't have, at that point, you need to ask yourself whether you will spend your time to learn new skills and knowledge. A few careers require specialized skills or affirmations. You are not willing to outfit yourself with new skills, how might you begin another career?

3: Spend your time to find out additional about the career you like

You may surmise that being a veterinarian is a career loaded with fun. Do you honestly find out the job extension and obligations of this expert? Without getting nitty-gritty data about a career, you may make the wrong judgment. Try not to judge a book by its cover. Specific jobs look straightforward however when you are in the actual situation; you may find that the jobs are tiring and distressing. Keeping in mind the end goal to dodge yourself from settling on the wrong choice, you are encouraged to talk with people in the critical field to share their encounters.

4: Attend career talk or search for the mentor

If you are the crisp graduate from school or college, it is continuously helpful for you to attend a career talk. Like this, you can have brief comprehension about the job extents of different careers. It will be an education for you. In the meantime, if you have no certainty to begin another career, searching for a solid mentor is basic. Let the mentor manage you in the original working condition.

Pick Your Mentors Wisely

You've begun your own home-based business, and you're excited about the likely outcomes. You have dreams of squaring away your home, venturing to the far corners of the planet, pristine autos stopped in the carport, spending quality time with your family all while your PC works like a robot all day and all night producing pay.

If you've been grinding away for any period, you've most likely found that it isn't precisely straightforward. It required diligent work, time and money and all the more fundamentally, a knowledge of what works, what doesn't work, what to spend money on and what not to spend money.

Enter the mentors.

You'll find them on each discussion gathering, you'll get various messages from them, and you'll keep running crosswise over them all alone as you make your way through the internet. Getting out like festival sideshow peddlers, they line the boulevards of the internet and forcefully vie for your consideration, apparently with honest intentions and your best interest on a fundamental level.

Be that as it may, what who truly needs to encourage you and who exceptionally needs to help themselves to a portion of your well-deserved money? Knowing the distinction between the two can genuinely spare you a great deal of time, dissatisfaction, and money, also your poise and sentiments of selling out once you understand what has happened.

Choosing the right mentor.

1. "I've made a fortune and simply need to help other people now." It is an infrequent occasion undoubtedly that somebody has quite recently made so much money that they feel like they should give back and need to help other people to succeed. This one is somewhat straightforward, yet people get bulldozed by it every day. Simply take a gander at the success of the late night infomercials if you need verification of this system. So how would you know whether you are the fortunate beneficiary of that one of every a billion authentic "needing to give back" success story? Does their help include your separating with some money? Do the greater part of the destinations they allude you to contain joins with their referral code? These are signs that they need to make a quick buck before you lose all expectation and bomb as generally do. It is a major market, and there is certainly those that go after those simply coming into the "work from home" business.

Some people honestly do get a kick out of the chance to help other people, and you will see that they regularly will allude you to a site with no referral code, so they don't benefit from their exhort. They usually will propose a free apparatus rather than one that will cost you money or if nothing else to one of the lesser costly ones which will carry out the job similarly and also one they could have sent you to with a referral connect and made themselves a decent commission.

2. Discussion Board Experts are there every step of the way. They quickly answer your inquiries and appear to be most useful, however, what amount do you honestly think about them. Is it accurate to say that they

are as successful as they persuade? To what extent have they been in business for themselves. Similarly, as harming as the ones who are attempting to exploit your aspirations are those that posture as specialists and which you are probably going to put your confidence in and follow, sometimes following them right down the path to disappointment.

In the ten or more years I've worked online for myself, I have seen it again and again. One day a man signs up and presents themselves as being new and merely beginning and half a month later you will see them offering advice on getting to be successful when they haven't made a dime yet. There is no simple answer. However, a couple of things should be possible to in any event encourage a bit.

Most discussion boards offer a search work; you can utilize this and search by the client. Change the choices to examine the distance back to the extent that it will and search for a "board mentors" first posts. You can get thought of when they began and followed them up until the present. Is it safe to say that they were griping merely a week ago because at that point haven't possessed the capacity to make any money? Is it accurate to say that they were asking a similar inquiry three days prior that they just responded in due order regarding you? Provided that this is true, you might get second-hand advice.

3. Did you approach your "mentor" or did they contact you? On the off chance that they've made an individual effort to search you out and offer their help, you ought to in any event keeps your monitor up and be attentive.

It isn't intended to make you non-trusting of everyone but instead to enable you to open your eyes and utilize alert and trustworthiness before choosing to follow somebody indiscriminately down one of the paths above. While choosing your mentors, use due tirelessness. Investigate them and their destinations. Search their names in the search motors, complete a who is on the spaces and check whether everything is arranging to be valid and exact. Do searches on the discussion to perceive what others need to say in regards to them and particularly their successes following the given advice of your conceivable mentor.

CONCLUSION

Career mentors get the self-gratification of realizing that he or she can help career growth and also help a company or association keep on replenishing gifted representatives. A career mentor might be hard to find at first, yet once you have one, they will be an essential device for your business advancement. Most abnormal state business administrators will both complimented and regarded if you request that they be your mentor. Odds are, they had someone helping them en route to the best, and will be cheerful to pass the support onto someone else! You could achieve a lasting change in peoples' demeanors, expel inabilities to think straight and help to dig profound into his particular mind to find answers for the issues, which she/he till now accepted never existed! In short, is the significance of being a mentor. Remember that mentoring is tied in with sharing experience and aptitude in a way that benefits both of the participants and in this way builds and reinforce the charitable sector all in all. As philanthropic professionals build up their leadership skills, it will be essential to fuse best practices into each mentoring relationship. Most successful people have sought a mentor at various times in their career. Many executives continue to find mentors long into their well-established jobs.

www.ingramcontent.com/pod-product-compliance
Lightning Source LLC
Chambersburg PA
CBHW030505220526
45464CB00006B/2667